I Teach,
I Touch
The Future

Connie

God bless

Phil. 4:13

I Teach,
I Touch
The Future

GARRE LaGRONE

Illustrated by
MATT LaGRONE

PUBLISHED BY

Destiny Consulting Group

Published by Destiny Consulting Group
A Division of Destiny Enterprises

D E S 9 2 5 5 6

To order extra copies of this book contact:

Destiny Consulting Group
P.O. Box 50127
Amarillo, Texas 79159
806-355-3357
email: teachtex@arn.net

Visit our web site at: *www.iteachkids.com*

"The greatest thing we can ever accomplish in this lifetime is to have been a positive influence in the life of a child."

-G.L.

Dedicated to

Mr. Oscar Hinger
Mrs. Eloise Burgess
Mrs. Kathryn McBride
Mrs. Alma Perkins
Mrs. Billie Keith
Mrs. Sue Hooper
Mrs. Pauline Brown
Mr. Ronnie Gordon
Mrs. Edith Priddy
Mrs. Beth Posey
Mrs. Jane Westberry
Mrs. Ada Crager
Mr. R.D. Wheelock
Mrs. Lillian Graham
Mr. Bryce Slack
Mr. Carroll Killingsworth
Mr. W. V. "Willie" McAlpin
Ms. Bess Brillhart
Mr. Louis Tversky
Mr. Earl Clardy
Mr. Dave Corley
Mr. Ron Mills
Mr. V.J. Duncan
Mrs. Mary Beth Ford
and
Dr. Derl Brooks

Thank you for making a difference in my life.

Contents

x

Acknowledgments

This book has taken almost two years from conception to completion. I am grateful to have had the opportunity to write and compile this material. It has been both a pleasure and a challenge. I am so proud to be called a teacher and I hope these writings will encourage and inspire other educators. I would like to acknowledge the following:

First and foremost I thank the Lord for salvation, and for so richly blessing my life.

My wife Brenda, you are my best friend and I thank you for your unbelievable love and support during this project, and in everything else I do. Thank you for your patience and support, and for your understanding for the many late hours and all the times I let dinner get cold. Also for all the proof reading and grammar checks. My love and respect to you always, you're the greatest!

My son Matt, thank you for lending your God-given talent to this project. You made it all the more special for me. I am so proud of you and I love you more than words can explain! You have a tremendous future ahead of you, so reach for the stars!

My daughter Hilleary, for the proof reading and moral support during this project. I hope you will gain a blessing from these words as you pursue your future in teaching. You are an inspiration and Christian role model to me and so many others. I love you dearly!

My step-son Stephen, I thank you for your positive attitude about life and for making a wonderful difference in mine!

To my sister Ginger Tucker, thank you for encouragement, guidance and support. You are a consummate professional.

To Jeanne Denton, thank you for your help in editing and proof reading my atrocious grammar.

To the teachers and educators listed on the dedication page of this book, I thank you for your years of dedicated service and sincere commitment to making a difference in the lives of children, because I was one of those children. Respect and admiration to you all forever.

To you, the teacher reading this book, I sincerely and humbly thank you for what you do. You are the most crucial cog in the most important wheel in our society. These poems, songs and stories are for you. This book is my small way of recognizing those of you who share the most important responsibility on earth...educating our children.

And last but not least, I thank the two greatest teachers I know... my mother and dad. They never checked roll, they never had a classroom and they never graded a paper, but they taught the most valuable lessons we ever learned, because they taught by example, with love, care and discipline, which is how all children learn...from the heart.

-G.L.

Introduction

The words held within this book are intended to inspire, motivate, entertain and show appreciation for educators.

Long after the lockers are empty and the hallways are clear, the impact you have on your students will be determined more by who you are than by what you teach. Teaching is about character and is a labor of love guided by hands of compassion. No other profession on earth can lay claim to the work of teachers.

Each of us can look back at our childhood and confirm that the person who made the biggest difference in our life, excluding our parents and grand-parents, was more than likely not a lawyer, a doctor, a banker, an accountant, a politician or a movie star...but a teacher.

Teachers are the one sector of our society most deserving of praise, admiration and appreciation. In the words of Lee Iacocca, *"In a completely rational society the best of us would aspire to be teachers."* I think the best of us are.

1
Visionary

The teacher said to the students,

"Come to the edge."

The students replied,

"We might fall."

The teacher again said,

"Come to the edge."

The students said,

"It's too high."

"Come to the edge!"

the teacher demanded.

The students came.

The teacher pushed them...

and they flew.

I Am a Teacher

I am a teacher, so proud to be,
Molding lives and shaping dreams.
On a mission of the heart,
With a vision to impart.

Helping students to succeed,
To be the best they can be.
Teaching values, integrity and truth,
It's not a job, it's what I do.

Consistent and fair, I hope to be.
May my students learn these traits from me.
A guiding light to show the way,
For every child, every day.

And my wish, I have but one,
When my days on earth are done.
That those I've taught might earnestly say
I made their world a better place.

The First Day of School

The first day of school is upon us,
Another summertime is complete.
Posters and maps, tape and thumb tacks,
My classroom is tidy and neat.

With construction paper autumn leaves
Each bulletin board is in place.
This morning at eight they'll open the gate.
The fall term begins today.

New books are stacked on the counter,
Not a single binding is freyed.
The chalkboard is clean,
Bright shiney and green,
Not an ounce of dust in the tray.

Old Glory hangs high overhead.
She's seen many a child's first pledge.
With chairs in neat rows,
And a big shiny globe
I gather my thoughts at my desk.

Somehow I feel unready.
The morning bell has just rung.
It's always this way.
Each year on this day.
What is it I've left undone?

I pray for wisdom and patience,
But most of all the latter.
May I start in September
And the whole year remember,
Children are really what matter.

Lord, be with this teacher.
May I be fair in my rule.
Let my enthusiasm be
The same in late spring
As it is on the first day of school.

If I change one single life...
then what I do is all worth while

-G.L.

I Teach, I Touch The Future

I teach kids to read and write,
Add, subtract, multiply and divide,
Nouns and verbs, science and history.

But you know, I teach so much more
Each day they come through my door.
For they learn so much...just watching me.

I teach, I touch the future.
Oh Lord, let my life light the way.
Not for glory fortune or fame,
My reward is "the difference I make".
I teach, I touch the future.... everyday.

Let me teach them "honesty",
"Right from wrong" and "integrity".
Give me the strength to do my part.
And if I change one single life,
Then what I do is all worth while.
Because, when they learn...
Children learn from the heart.

Yes, I teach, I touch the future.
Oh Lord, let my life light the way.
Not for glory fortune or fame,
My reward is "the difference I make".
I teach, I touch the future.... everyday.

Lyrics of the song *I Teach, I Touch the Future*
written by Garre LaGrone, Brenda-Scott LaGrone and Ginger Tucker
from the album *Thank a Teacher* by Garre LaGrone
For more information about the album contact
Destiny Consulting Group 888-689-3123

By Definition

teach-er (tē′ chĕr), **n,** one who teaches others; instructor.

-Webster

teach-er (tē′ chĕr), **n,** one who imparts vision, builds self-esteem, shapes dreams and molds character.

-LaGrone

Prayer in School

The law now states we cannot pray
In our schools in this country today.
It seems to me, very odd
In a Nation founded under God.

Who are "they", this radical few
To draw such boundaries around me and you.
For no law can stop compassion and love
From asking for guidance from up above

So each day I'll send, from my desk,
Many silent Heaven bound requests.
And special blessings I will ask
For each student in my class.

My appeal, I'll keep to my self,
And never burden anyone else.
I'll respect our constitutional rule.
But, as long as I teach...
There'll be prayer in school.

A Tale of Two Cindys

During her first year as a classroom teacher Mrs. Beverly Grant learned an incredible lesson she would carry with her for the remainder of her 32 year teaching career.

The year was 1964 and Beverly was teaching at Mansfield High School, her Alma Mater. She felt a sense of pride and accomplishment for the opportunity to teach at her old school and she truly cared about her students. Teaching geography was a passion for Beverly.

The first few weeks of school had been fairly uneventful, except for a few minor ups and downs.

With her politeness and good nature Cindy Adkinson had made an impression on Mrs. Grant from the first day of school. Tall, pretty and clean cut she was the president of the Sophomore class and a starter on the girls volleyball team. Cindy was a well mannered and confident young lady.

Cindy Bingham, another one of Miss Grant's students, had made an impression as well. She had never caused any problems in class but had hardly said a word since school began. Her grade was bordering on failure and it was only the middle of September. She was just one of those invisible students.

Tuesday September 18th was parents night at Mansfield High and Beverly had worked late the night before to make the final preparations for the evening. She was a bit nervous about meeting some of the parents. Mansfield was a college town and many of the parents of her students taught at the local university.

Parents began arriving around 7:00 P.M. Beverly enjoyed sharing refreshments and visiting about each student with their parents. She was very pleased with the turnout.

A steady flow of visitors continued until around 8:15 when Beverly said good-bye to what she thought was the last parent when a lady walked into her room. She was dressed very conservatively and had a kind smile.

"Hello, I'm Cindy's mother." said the lady. "I'm so sorry I'm just getting here, but I worked late. You must be Mrs. Grant, I've heard so much about you."

"Yes, I am", said Beverly, "It is so nice to meet you. Let me tell you about that Cindy of yours. She is a wonderful young lady and a true joy to have in class. If all students were like her this world would be a much better place."

Beverly went on, "Cindy does excellent work, and she is always so polite and mannerly. I know you must be very proud."

"Yes, yes I am," said Cindy's mother. "She says so many nice things about you also."

They walked around the classroom and talked a short while longer.

"Well, it's late and I won't keep you any longer." said Cindy's mother. "I just wanted to come by and introduce myself. Please let me know if there is anything I can do to help you with Cindy."

They said goodnight and she walked out the door.

The next day in the teacher's lounge Beverly was visiting with Robert Blake, the Choir director, about parents night and how well it had gone.

"Oh, I met Cindy Adkinson's mother last night," Beverly explained, "She is so nice."

"What?" asked Robert with a puzzled look. "That can't be."

"What do you mean?" asked Beverly

"Well," said Robert, "Cindy Adkinson's mother died of cancer two years ago."

"I'm confused," said Beverly. "A lady came into my room and said, I'm Cindy's moth...."

Then it hit her. The lady she had visited with was Cindy Bingham's mother.

"All the things I told her were about Cindy Adkinson," Beverly said with a worried look.

"If it was all positive stuff, I wouldn't worry about it." said Robert.

What transpired in the next few months was quit amazing.

Cindy Adkinson continued to be the bright energetic and promising student that she was from the beginning. But Mrs. Grant witnessed an incredible metamorphosis. All of the positive words of praise and encouragement she had said to Cindy Bingham's mother had been relayed to her. Cindy (Bingham that is) gradually began participating in class at a higher level. Her grades came up to the mid 80's in all her classes over the course of the year. With continued praise and encouragement from Mrs. Grant, she earned an 87 in geography for the year. Her classmates noticed a tremendous change in her self-esteem and confidence.

Her Junior year, Cindy Bingham ran for student council representative and was elected. She also became a member of the debate team. The following year she graduated with a 82.7 overall average.

Cindy Bingham is now married with two children. She and her husband own their own business in Arizona. Every year, to this day, she sends a Christmas card and makes a phone call to the one person she says made the biggest difference in her life...her dear friend and mentor Mrs. Beverly Grant, who retired in 1996.

We have such power over the lives of the children we teach. For many of them we are their visionaries. And as Mrs. Grant found out... A little praise goes a long way!

Tireless dedication
Endless effort
Attitude of praise
Character of integrity
Honest commitment
Enthusiasm for the profession
Role model

-G.L.

No Other Profession

Who else is in the business
Of helping dreams come true,
Building self esteem and character
With all you say and do?

Always there to help, you dedicate yourself
To molding boys and girls.
My friend your occupation's
The most important in the world.

No other profession changes more lives.
No other profession instills more pride.
Through adolescent eyes
You're a guiding light,
A beacon down life's road.
Your work is like
No other profession that I know.

You never do receive
The praise that you deserve,
Still you carry on with dignity,
Never paid quite what you're worth.

Hard work and dedication
Day in and day out,
With all the lives you've touched
As the jewels in your crown.

No other profession changes more lives.
No other profession instills more pride.
Through adolescent eyes
You're a guiding light,
A beacon down life's road.
Your work is like
No other profession that I know.

Lyrics of the song *No Other Profession*

written by Garre LaGrone and Brenda-Scott LaGrone

from the album *Thank a Teacher* by Garre LaGrone

For more information about the album contact

Destiny Consulting Group 888-689-3123

To The First-Year Teacher

Your schooling is finally over.
But your learning has just begun.
Good teachers grow day by day as they go.
Your training will never be done.

Always teach with humility.
Take advice from mentors around you.
Never loose your wit or your confidence,
You know more than you think you do.

Stay away from negative people.
Keep your enthusiasm high.
There'll be mistakes all along the way
But don't ever lose that spark in your eye.

There are things you'll need to know
That didn't come with your degree.
For teaching is and art fine-tuned by the heart
With compassion and sincerity.

Keep your sense of humor
Have fun from time to time
Help your class learn to laugh
It's medicine for the mind.

Get to know your students
Share hobby's and things that you do.
As you go let the children know
They are special...but so are you.

Be leery of that place
They call the "Teacher's lounge".
Use extra care and run from there
If they're putting children down.

You won't get the respect you deserve
From our society.
So respect yourself and remember well
Just why you chose to teach.

For no one else on earth
Has a more important role.
You are a "Teacher", and a "Believer"
A true professional.

Never be afraid
Of blunders you're bound to make.
Take them all with a grain of salt,
But, learn from your mistakes.

Be proud of every child
Who walks into your room.
Make learning fun and help each one
Succeed in all they do.

Don't worry if kids don't like you.
A"buddy" is not what they need.
Always be kind and do what is right
And a "lifetime friend" you will be.

*To reach children's minds a teacher
must capture their hearts.*

The Power Of The Heart

Tender enough to make
A grown man cry,
Yet strong enough to make
A house a home.
It's warm enough to send
Chills up your spine,
But cold enough to tell you
Right from wrong.

It can blind true love,
It can light up the dark.
In this world
There's nothing stronger than
The Power of the Heart

It can change a new mother's pain
Into tears of joy.
And it shapes the life
Of every girl and boy.
Even when it's broken,
It still works like a charm.
Yes it's true,
There's nothing stronger than...
The Power of the Heart

The Power of the Heart,
Oh, The Power of the Heart!
It can conquer the impossible,
Work miracles
And heal the deepest scars.
There's nothing we couldn't do
If we'd only use
The Power of the Heart!

We could join all the hands of the world,
And make this a better place.
We could move mountains of doubt,
And put a smile on every human face.
We'd have peace at last,
If we just knew where to start.
It's so simple my friends,
It all begins with
The Power of the heart.

The Power of the Heart,
Oh, The Power of the Heart!
It can conquer the impossible,
Work miracles
And heal the deepest scars.
There's nothing we couldn't do
If we'd only use
The Power of the Heart!

© Copyright 1998 Garre LaGrone

Lyrics of the song *The Power of the Heart*
written by Garre LaGrone
from the album *Thank a Teacher* by Garre LaGrone
For more information about the album contact
Destiny Consulting Group 1-888-689-3123

2
Mentor

May I teach children

not just to read... but absorb,

not just to write... but create,

not just to look... but explore,

not just to touch... but feel,

not just to hear... but listen,

and not just to exist... but live.

-G.L.

Thank A Teacher

My success, and my beliefs
I owe to those chosen to teach.
My heart's filled with gratitude!

When I really stop and think about it,
"All I know", I'd be lost without it.
I'm giving credit where it's due.

Thank a teacher for just taking the time.
Thank a teacher for improving your life.
Everybody takes it all for granted,
But we're only harvesting what they planted.
Yeah, thank a teacher!

I'm so obliged for all I've learned.
I'm indebted for their concern.
I could never repay all that I owe.

I'm so grateful they love what they do.
They touch the future, yes it's true.
So I'm letting my appreciation show.

Thank a teacher for just taking the time.
Thank a teacher for improving your life.
Everybody takes it all for granted,
But we're only harvesting what they planted.
Yeah, thank a teacher!

Lyrics of the song *Thank a Teacher*
written by Garre LaGrone
from the album *Thank a Teacher* by Garre LaGrone
For more information about the album contact
Destiny Consulting Group 888-689-3123

Young Eyes

You can lecture every day,
Rant 'n rave and pontificate,
With vast amounts of knowledge to impart.

But, be mindful of what you do and say.
Choose your words with care each day.
For nothing speaks as loud as who you are.

Don't abuse the lives in your hands,
Or the power that you have.
No one plays the crucial role you do.

Let your message always be
One of truth and integrity.
For you see...young eyes are watching you.

Joey's Wish

A poem from a principal to his staff

We asked our kids,
"If you had one wish,"
"What would that one wish be?"

Most girls and boys
Wished for new toys,
Candy and a lot of silly things.

But one little boy
Filled my heart with joy.
And reminded me of the difference we make.

Little Joey said,
"I wish every kid
Could have a teacher just like Mrs. Blake."

With just the right mix of chalk and challenge
a teacher can change lives.

Blue Ribbon Speller

A story shared with me by a teacher from Austin, Texas:

Several years ago a third grade girl was asked to spell the word *teacher* in her schools annual spelling bee. With a happy smile the pretty little girl stepped up to the microphone in her curls and bows, and without hesitation said loud and clear,

"teacher, S - A - I - N - T, teacher"

For Jenny

A few weeks back we started
A fund-raiser at our school.
Our kids were collecting money
To help a little girl.

Jenny Young has Leukemia
She is in Mrs. Butler's class.
All my kids were saddened by
The fate of this young lass.

My students got together
And decorated a can.
To collect donations,
They had a special plan.

On the day we passed the can around
The kids took out their change.
Clink clank, clink clank into the can,
They were so proud of what they gave.

But there was one who gave
Much more than all the rest.
Tommy Fields had sixteen bills
Lying on his desk.

I must confess I was surprised
When he began to count.
And I worried where young Tommy
Had come by such an amount.

I'm ashamed to admit
The thoughts that I did think.
I had visions of robbery and theft,
Or a broken piggy bank.

"I've saved all my money", Tommy said
"Every nickel, dime and penny.
Each day at lunch I went outside
And said prayer for Jenny."

I learned a priceless lesson
On that blessed day.
About a special sacrifice
And the gift a little boy gave.

For Tommy hadn't eaten lunch
Since a week ago last Wednesday.
Eleven days he had saved,
And he gave it all for Jenny.

Teaching is a work of heart.

It's All About The Kids

We must be ever mindful,
In our noble quest,
To strive each day and collaborate
To help children do their best.

We're not in private practice.
Personal gain is not our concern.
Our ultimate goal, as we all know,
Is to help all children learn.

On our glorious mission
Let us not forget,
It's not about you
And it's not about me.
It's all about the kids.

A Pat On The Back

I had a visitor at school today
Who stopped to say hello.
She walked in and said, "Remember me?
You taught me years ago."

It took a moment, then I knew
This woman, once a child,
Was Sarah Parker, all grown up,
I said, "It's been a while."

We talked a while and shared some laughs
Of all the days gone by.
Then the words she said to me,
How they changed my life.

Here for her class reunion,
Can it be? It's been ten years.
She shared a special story
As my eyes welled up with tears.

She said she wouldn't be alive
If it hadn't been for me.
I must have had a puzzled look
When I said "What do you mean?"

She said "Do you remember
Our second-period class?"
I had to think, but it came to me,
She sat way in the back.

Quiet, subdued and withdrawn,
Never causing any grief,
She came and went every day.
Her work was always neat.

She said, "You know, you saved my life."
I thought, "How can it be."
"You made me feel worthwhile," she said.
"You were always praising me."

"I was mistreated at home," she explained.
"Neglected and abused.
I thought I was a worthless child,
But I learned differently from you."

"One day in class you came to me
To check my science lab
You said I was a gifted child,
Then gave me a gentle pat."

She said, "I'd contemplated suicide
Almost every day.
Thanks to you, I crossed that bridge.
Now I'm here to say."

"You gave me self-esteem
And a belief in myself.
You told me words I'd never heard
From anybody else."

She said, "I left that living hell called home
And worked my way through school.
I know I can make it in this world,
There's nothing I can't do."

We exchanged a hug and said good-bye.
She disappeared down the hall,
As I thought to myself, "a pat on the back?"
I don't remember it at all.

*Children are the only future mankind
has... teach them well.*

For Pete's Sake

He's just a little boy,
He has so much to learn.
Won't you teach him well,
Show him your concern.

Don't look down on him,
For he looks up to you.
Show him that you care,
With everything you say and do.

And for Pete's sake,
Help him understand.
For Pete's sake,
Lend a guiding hand.
For you just might be the light
That helps him find the way.
Teach from the heart
For Pete's sake.

Yes, he's just a little boy,
He's special can't you see.
Praise him every day,
Teach him to believe.

Please encourage him,
He has so many dreams.
Help him do his best,
Whatever that might be.

So for Pete's sake,
Help him understand.
For Pete's sake,
Lend a guiding hand.

For you just might be the light
That helps him find the way.
Teach from the heart
For Pete's sake.

Lyrics of the song *For Pete's Sake*
written by Garre LaGrone, Brenda-Scott LaGrone and Ginger Tucker
from the album *Thank a Teacher* by Garre LaGrone
For more information about the album contact
Destiny Consulting Group 1-888-689-3123

Katie's Dad

I watched them coming down the hall.
He stood well over six feet tall,
And her hair was tied up neatly with a bow.

I said, "Well, who is this fine young lady?"
She said, "Hello ma'am, my name is Katie."
Then she looked up, not wanting him to go.

She had an apprehensive look.
One arm clutched her new notebook,
With the other clinging tightly to his hand.

He said, "Good morning Mrs. Reeves,
I'm Katie's Dad, excuse us please."
Then kneeling, gently pulled her close to him.

I heard him, as I stepped away,
"Katie this is your big day.
Trust me, I know you'll do just fine."

He said, "I remember my first day,
So I know you're going to love this place.
And your teacher, Mrs. Reeves, she's very nice."

"She cares about you just like us.
And I know she's someone you can trust.
I wouldn't leave you if it wasn't so."

"I know it's hard, because it's something new,
But Mom will be here for you this afternoon
And we'll talk about your day when I get home."

He said, "It doesn't seem that long ago
I was in your shoes, you know.
I was unsure and frightened, just like you."

"But I found out, here at school,
Learning things is really cool.
You'll do great, there's nothing you can't do."

"Okay honey that's your room.
Mrs. Reeve's will take good care of you.
This will be the greatest day you've ever had."

He winked and smiled then walked away.
I took her hand as I prayed,
"Lord let me live up to the praise of Katie's Dad."

*How children come to us is no excuse
for how they leave us.*

The Harvest

Deep in the richest soil
I'll plant ambitious seeds.
Although, a bountiful harvest
I may never see.

I'll cultivate success and pride,
And pull the weeds of doubt.
Young minds will reap what I sow,
Let the rain of wisdom come down.

With concern and compassion
I'll care for every seed.
May my crops grow tall with pride
And all their roots run deep.

When the autumn comes
And my labor is complete.
The difference that I made
Is the harvest that I'll reap.

My Class

When children come into my class
I treat them special there.
I make them feel important
With compassion, love and care.

I try to be consistent
And fair in every way,
To each and every child,
Each and every day.

I greet them every morning
And send them home with a smile.
My goal each day for my class
Is success for every child.

I pray my students will look back
When all the years have past,
With many a fond memory
Of being in my class.

3
Role Model

If we don't model what we teach...

we are teaching something else.

The Call

They call you teacher.
You are a special breed.
It is a calling,
A noble duty indeed.

No greater appointment
Could be received.
For you cultivate and plant
The most important seeds.

You answered the call,
Always giving your all.
You dedicate yourself
Like nobody else,
For you believe in the cause.
So glad that you do what you do.
Now just look at all
The people who are thankful
You answered the call.

We take for granted,
The work that you do.
Surely up in heaven's
A special place for you.
You guide the hands
Of fate and destiny
Through the door to the future,
For you hold the key.

You answered the call,
Always giving your all.
You dedicate yourself
Like nobody else,
For you believe in the cause.

So glad that you do what you do.
Now just look at all
The people who are thankful
You answered the call.

Lyrics of the song *The Call*

written by Garre LaGrone and Brenda-Scott LaGrone

from the album *Thank a Teacher* by Garre LaGrone

For more information about the album contact

Destiny Consulting Group 1-888-689-3123

Nothing Like His Sister

First day of school he came to me.
Said his name was Billy Spencer.
I looked at him and thought, "Oh boy!"
He's nothing like his sister.

I'd heard about him in the lounge.
They said he was a prankster.
And that he'd never amount to anything.
He's nothing like his sister.

There's not a rule he didn't break.
He never learned to whisper.
They were right, he's quit a card.
He's nothing like his sister.

Yes, he was a pain at times,
Just like a little blister.
Proud, loud and confident.
He's nothing like his sister.

He never made the honor roll,
But he always called me mister.
He was not what I expected.
He's nothing like his sister.

Last day of school he said to me,
"I learned a lot, and I'm gonna miss ya."
I fought a tear as he said good-bye.
He's nothing like his sister.

Lord, thank you for this special child
And for making me a teacher.
Forgive me, please, for judging him.
He's nothing like his sister.

Children remember their teachers,
not methods and techniques.

Teacher's Prayer

Lord, let my words and my ways
Express my true concern
For children and their future,
If that is all they ever learn.

If I teach them just one thing,
Let it be appreciation
For their freedom, for their rights,
For this glorious nation.

Help me to remember Lord
With each and every day
Children learn so much more
From what I do than what I say.

When the final roll is called
And the bell rings my last day
May the lessons that I've taught
Make their world a better place.

Humor at School

"Humor is mankind's greatest blessing."
-Mark Twain

Some humorous school bulletins,
announcements and events.

Announcement heard over intercom

The flu is blamed for many absences this week
both by students and teachers. Keep those who
are sick of our school in your prayers.

From a Faculty Newsletter

During the absence of our Principal, Mr. Curry,
we enjoyed the rare treat of a great faculty
meeting with our Superintendent Mr. Sanders.

Our school nurses Mrs. Wade and Miss Lucero will be administering student inoculations in the cafeteria during 5th period today and tomorrow. There will be a station at the North and South sides of the cafeteria. Students will receive shots at both ends.

Teachers: We are currently taking up a collection to help pay for the new carpet in the lounge. Anyone who wants to do something on the carpet see Mr. Pierce in his office.

The Drama II class will present Shakespeare's Hamlet in the Auditorium this Thursday night at 7:00 P.M. All students and faculty members are invited to attend this tragedy.

Teachers who have small children and don't know it, the Student Council will offer baby sitting service in the library during the Faculty Banquet Tuesday night.

Mr. Blades (7th Grade Science) and Miss. Carter (8th Grade English) were married over spring-break, thus ending a five year friendship. Congratulations Mr. and Mrs. Blades!

Members of the FFA class entered animals in the Stock Show at the State Fair last week. Chad Martin took first prize, he had a cow.

Teachers: Effective April 5th, smoking will no longer be allowed in the school building. Please keep your butts outside.

Mr. O'Brien's Biology I classes will be taking a field trip to the Lake Urban Dam and Reservoir next month. The exact day and time will be announced as soon as Mr. O'Brien hears from the dam supervisor.

Announcement heard over intercom

"Good morning Lincoln High this is Coach Swartz. I want to commend the student body for the excellent turnout at the pep rally last night, the stadium was almost completely full of athletic supporters."

Announcement heard over intercom

To those 8th graders who have been helping teachers after school, your time and hard work are greatly appreciated. But yesterday there was an unsightly chalk mess left on the west side of our school building that has to be cleaned off by our custodians. Students DO NOT beat the erasers against the brick walls, please use your head!"

Conversation between student and teacher

Homer came into class one morning and said to his teacher, "Mrs. Pollard, I et seven pancakes for breakfast this morning."

"You mean ate, Homer." said Mrs. Pollard.

Homer thought for a second and then replied, "Maybe it was eight I et."

Mrs. Cynthia Lopez gave an emotional farwell speech at a retirement reception held in her honor last Tuesday evening in the commons. Mrs. Lopez is retiring after 35 years in the classroom. After her speech the High School choir sang "Hallelujah."

A story shared with me by a teacher from Pasadena, Texas

A Mother picked up her daughter after her first day of second grade. The mother asked, "How was your day honey?"

"Not too good," the little girl replied dejectedly.

"What do you mean?" asked her mother.

"Well," the little girl said, "Our teacher gave us this card to fill out this morning and I didn't know one of the answers, so she gave me an F in SEX."

From a faculty newsletter

Rob Freeman, our industrial arts teacher, caught a Lake record 11 lb. 9 0z. Large-mouth at Lake Redding. Rob's record setting ass will be on display in our trophy case all next week.

Great teachers teach children how to think... not what to think.

There's No "I" In "Team"

There's no "I" in "Team"
No room for words like "me"
Just "us", "ours" and "we"
It takes dedication and cooperation
If we are to succeed.

There's no "I" in "Team"
Make sure we all agree.
We've got to have congeniality.
Children learn much better
When we work together.
There's no "I" in "Team"

A "major" Discovery

One day while teaching her ninth grade Biology class Susan Lane learned a phenomenon of education she will never forget. She had been teaching a unit on the human muscular system. Her students were truly engaged in learning and were enjoying the topic thoroughly. This particular afternoon she was quizzing her class and reviewing certain muscles of the body and their *scientific names*. The students were to have a test over the material the following day.

Mrs. Lane proceeded around the room randomly asking questions.

Pointing at her own thigh, she asked a girl in the second row, who was waving her hand frantically, "Okay Amy, what is the *Scientific name* of this muscle?"

The young girl stood quickly with confidence, "*Rectus femoris*" she said, without hesitation.

"Very good", said Mrs. Lane, thinking to herself, "I can see her now, "scrubbing up" for surgery."

Her next question was for Eric, who always knew his stuff.

"Eric," she said with a professor like tone, "This muscle", pointing to the back of her upper arm, "what is it's *scientific name*?"

There was a brief pause...then it came.

"*T r i c e p s   b r a c h i i*?" he said, stretching out the words in an almost questioning way.

"That's correct Eric, excellent!" said Mrs. Lane.

"Who knows the name of these muscles?" Mrs. Lane asked, as she pointed to her upper chest.

"I know, I know Mrs. Lane!" came a cry from the back of the room.

"Oh my Lord, it couldn't be", she thought to herself...but yes it was. It was Eddie Fraiser, who's class participation was usually, to say the least, non-academic. Standing up over his desk waving his hand wildly he yelled again,

"I know Mrs. Lane, I know."

She wasn't sure she wanted to hear his answer, but he was the only student in class with his hand up.

"Y-e-s E-d-d-i-e?", Mrs. Lane asked, as she drew a deep breath.

He never wavered as he stood and blurted out *"Pectoralis major!"*

A deep sigh of relief rushed out from the depths of her soul, and a look of amazement fell over the entire class.

"E-E-Excellent Eddie!" she exclaimed, after a brief pause. "You studied, way to go! I am so proud of you."

"No, I didn't study Mrs. Lane.", Eddie explained. "That one's easy to remember. You know why?"

"N-N-No Eddie, why?", asked Mrs. Lane apprehensively.

"Because breasts are major!" he shouted, as the class erupted in laughter.

She had to bite her lip to keep from joining in the chorus, but for the first time all year Mrs. Lane was speechless.

Saved by the bell, she urged her students to study for tomorrow's test, as they filed out the door, most of them still chuckling.

Mrs. Lane had always heard, that when you teach something mixed with emotion, it sinks in. Amen! Not a single student missed that question on the test the following day.

It is not the calling of teachers to
see through their students...
But to see their students through.

Making a Difference

A man was walking on an isolated stretch of beach just after high tide. As far as he could see down the shore-line were strewn what seemed to be millions of starfish left behind after the ocean had receded.

Taken by the solitude of the moment he was awestruck by nature's way. It seemed he was the only human alive when he noticed a person, some distance down the shore, walking back and forth between the beach and the water.

As he approached it became apparent that the person was an elderly woman clad in an old sweat shirt and cotton pants rolled up to the knees. She was returning the helpless starfish to the sea one by one. Carefully and methodically she would cradle each one in a bed of sand and wade out into the tide and release each delicate creature. The morning walker was puzzled by the old woman's curious course of action.

"Why are you doing that?" he asked loudly.

She just smiled.

"You'll never make a difference." He exclaimed. "There must be millions of them along this beach", he yelled as she walked by again, smiling.

"You'll never make a difference!", he shouted again above the ocean's roar.

She smiled again, bent down, picked up another starfish, waded into the water again and gently returned another creature to it's ocean home. She walked by the man again and said proudly,

"I made a difference for that one," as she picked up another one and headed for the surf.

-Unknown

Teacher's Pet

Jody is a bright young boy
He made an A on his test.
I acknowledged his hard work
And his accomplishment.

Sally wrote a great report
About the Indians of the plains.
I told her she was gifted,
I gave her high acclaims.

Jason won the blue ribbon
At our school spelling bee.
I praised him for his effort,
A talented lad indeed.

Bobby is no different,
Although a challange at times.
He's not a model student,
Sometimes he tries my mind.

He has so much potential,
So many paths he cannot see.
If someone doesn't show the way
How will he succeed?

Other teachers say
He's not like all the rest.
I disagree, for it's up to me
To help him find success.

He may not make the honor roll
Or do outstanding work.
But it's my responsibility
To show him what he's worth.

May I be fair in every way,
And let him see it in my smile.
Lord, help my mission clearly be
Success for every child.

Help me make him feel important,
And never let him forget...
That in my class every child I teach
Is the teacher's pet.

*Challenge your students to pursue a
lifetime of learning.*

Teach Children to Succeed

A ritual I have used for years is to write a "Success Phrase" on my board and let it remain there for the entire week. The first day of the week we spend a few minutes at the beginning of each class period discussing the phrase for that week. These positive anecdotes are great for stimulating and inspiring students minds and for promoting greater insight and personal growth toward a successful life. On Friday I have each student put the phrase into his or her own words and keep them in their personal Success Journal. The following pages contain some of the "Success Phrases" I've used through the years. Use them to challenge children to succeed!

Mistakes are stepping stones to success.

The only time success comes before
work is in the dictionary.

Success comes in cans... I cans.

Practice does not make perfect.
Only perfect practice makes perfect.

Success is a four letter word... WORK

There are no stupid questions...
questions get answers.

People who will lie for you, will lie to you.

There are those who make things happen, those who watch things happen, and those who wonder, "what happened?"

The value of a man should be seen in what he gives and not in what he is able to receive.

It seems there is never enough time to do it right, but there is always enough time to do it over.

You'll never get ahead of anyone as long as you are trying to get even.

If you think you can, or if you think you can't... you're right.

Never let what you can't do interfere with what you can do.

"If we did all the things we are capable of doing,
we would literally astound ourselves."

-Thomas Edison

To finish sooner...take your time.

The greatest mistake you can make is to be afraid
of making a mistake.

If you think education is expensive, wait until
you see what ignorance will cost you.

Avoid shortcuts, they always take
more time in the long run.

Keeping up is always easier than catching up.

If someone says something unkind about you,
live your life so that no one will believe them.

The best way to get rid of an enemy
is to make him your friend.

It's not whether you get knocked down,
it's whether you get up.

It is easier to stay out of trouble
than to get out of trouble.

If you keep doing what you're doing
you'll keep getting what you're getting.

There are two types of fools:
Those who trust everyone and
those who trust no one.

If you tried to do something and failed,
you are far better off than if you had tried
to do nothing and succeeded.

If you keep looking back,
you are bound to run into trouble.

Worrying about *what's* right is always more
important than worrying about *who's* right.

Success comes to those who make things happen,
not to those who let things happen.

If you aren't happy with what you have now,
what makes you think you'll be happier with more.

If you wait for all conditions to be perfect before
you take action... you'll never take action

Make a positive difference in someone's
life every day.

Success is a state of mind.

What your mind can conceive and believe
your mind can achieve.

Success is the sum of small efforts,
repeated day in and day out.

It's not what happens to you that matters,
it's what happens to what happens
to you that counts.

A house of success is built one brick at a time.

Watch for big problems. They are sometimes
disguised as big opportunities.

Success is a journey...not a destination

The only limits are, as always, those of vision.

There is a time in the life of every problem when it is big enough to see, yet small enough to solve.

Good friends are good for your health.

Without music, life is a journey through a desert.

Think big thoughts... but relish small pleasures.

"Success is how high you bounce
when you hit bottom."

-Gen. George Patton

The manner in which a gift is given is
worth more than the gift.

If you want to test your memory,
try to remember what you were worried
about one year ago today.

I've suffered through many a tragedy in my
life...most of which never happened.

Knowledge is gained by learning; trust by doubt;
skill by practice; and love by love.

Have a genuine interest in people and be kind to
them...kindness is everything.

You never learn anything by talking. You only
learn by asking questions
and listening.

A man's greatest strength develops at the point
where he overcomes
his greatest weakness.

Good luck is hard to detect - it looks so much like
something you've earned.

Our wisdom lies solely in
the knowledge of our ignorance.

-Socrates

A cloudy day is no match for a sunny disposition.

If you want to truly understand
something, try to change it.

A stumble may prevent a fall.

"The moment of victory is much to short
to live for that and nothing else."

-Martina Navratilova

The more original a discovery, the more
obvious it seems afterwards.

Perseverance is not a long race;
but many short races one after another.

Focus on where you're going,
not where you've been.

Success is learned...then earned.

Mischievous Kids

Thank God for mischievous kids,
Those clever spunky little ones.
Kids who don't steer
Down the paths of their peers
And who march to a different drum.

Thank God for mischievous kids,
Those creative spontaneous tikes
Who can't help but express
Their ornery
And challenge our patience at times.

Thank God for mischievous kids,
Who aren't afraid of making mistakes.
Kids who lose books
And don't have pretty looks
But who always make their own way.

Thank God for mischievous kids,
Those delightfully different boys and girls.
When it's all said and done
They'll be the ones
Who'll make a real difference in the world.

I once heard someone say,
"I'm just a teacher."

I replied,
"Yes, just the most important
job in the world!"

Who You Are

What you do is emotional work
Fused with passion, challenge and joy.
You play life's most important role.
Carefully guiding each girl and boy.

But it's not a job you see,
For what you do is of the heart.
Molding lives, shaping dreams,
A lifetime work of art.

No one else can lay claim
To the special work you do.
Heaven holds a grand reward
For a chosen few.

Quite content in your quest,
A mission of the heart.
It's your life, it's not a job.
A teacher...who you are.

Parents

They faithfully save egg cartons
And pimento cheese containers
For every classroom project,
And they never are complainers.

Those dedicated ones
Who volunteer for every cause,
Working every school event,
Never taking a pause.

They take off work on career day
To help the children see
The various jobs and professions
They might someday want to be.

The ones who give their time,
As precious as it is,
All for education
And the betterment of kids.

They come to every ball game
And cheer no matter what.
And win or lose they never gripe,
That really means a lot!

These extra special people,
Every dad and every mother,
Who always demonstrate concern
And commitment like no other.

The ones who help with homework
And check to see that it's right,
To insure their children
Understand their problems every night.

They praise us for the work we do,
And the difference that we make.
They appreciate a teacher's worth
And overlook our human mistakes.

They are models of integrity,
Truth and honesty.
Children learn much more from them
Than they do from me.

They're grateful that their kids love school
And they thank us for what we do.
Thank you Lord, for parents
Those special chosen few.

*May I teach my students
an appreciation for this incredible
existence called life.*

*Let my words and my
actions transmit a sense of fascination
and awe for this magnificent world
in which we live.*

You Taught Me

There is no higher calling,
for you touch young lives.

You impart a vision of the world
with your patience and care.

You light the pathway of life
with wisdom and understanding.

Because of your love and compassion
the world is a better place.

I can do all that I do...
because you taught me.

To Our School Secretary

Thank you Mrs. Byars
For the special work you do.
Our school is very lucky
To have a secretary like you.

Each morning children swarm you,
But you treat them like your own.
And you're always kind and dignified
To parents on the phone.

In all the years you've worked here
I've never heard you say
An angry or unpleasant word,
You always act the same.

You make our school a happy place
And the kids all think you're cool.
Mr. Warren is our Principal
But we all know you run the school.

So thank you Mrs. Byars
For the special work you do.
And don't ever underestimate
What children think of you.

Because when people ask me
Who my favorite teacher was.
I say, "Our Secretary, Mrs. Byars."
For you taught me oh so much.

Thank God For Mrs. Brown

Thank God for Mrs. Brown,
She taught me how to write.
Because of her, I can read.
Oh, how she changed my life.

She taught us all the presidents,
And our nation's song.
We learned the meaning of honesty.
She taught us right from wrong.

We learned about the weather,
And how the planets turn.
Our class went to the zoo one time.
She made it fun to learn.

She took us once to Africa
In a story about the Serengeti.
She even played baseball with us.
And we made a windmill out of glue and
spaghetti.

For thirty years she taught
Here in our little town,
My dad, my mom, my sister and me.
Thank God for Mrs. Brown.

She's no longer here with us,
But she lives within my heart.
Such a kind and giving soul,
In so many lives she played a part.

I often think about her
And wonder if she's smiling down,
Now that I'm a teacher.
Thank God for Mrs. Brown!

The moment you set foot in the classroom you are a role model... you have no choice.

Whether you choose to be a positive role model or a negative role model... that is your choice.

"Garre, your music and your message are Chicken Soup for my soul!"

Jack Canfield
#1 New York Times best-selling author of
Chicken Soup for the Soul

Thank a Teacher
Available on Compact Disc

ORDER YOURS TODAY!

$15.00 + 2.50 S/H

Destiny Consulting Group

P.O. Box 50127
Amarillo, Texas 79159
1-888-689-3123

Or order from our website www.iteachkids.com

Garre LaGrone

Garre LaGrone is an energetic, confident presenter and trainer who can make a positive difference for your staff. As an experienced communicator, having taught at both Jr. High and High School levels he brings enthusiasm and energy to his presentations. The presence he developed as an entertainer and performer while touring with country music star Lorrie Morgan is very evident when he is in front of an audience. Garre has combined his talent and love for music with his passion for education to offer dynamic and moving presentations that are having an incredible impact on educators throughout the country.

"Garre, keep up your great work. Your music and your message are Chicken Soup for my soul!"

Jack Canfield
#1 New York Times best-selling author of
Chicken Soup for the Soul

Garre facilitates the learning process by involving his audience. His skill at using everyday teaching situations, inspiring original songs, research-based content and humorous anecdotes to communicate his message makes each presentation or training unique, effective and fun! Arleen Belaire, Principal of Edgar Park Elementary School in El Paso, Texas noted, "What a positive impact your presentation has had on our faculty and staff. I have witnessed a renewal of commitment and joy for teaching. I know our children will reap the benefits of the time we spent with you."

"Through his music and message, Garre speaks to the heart, the soul and the intellect of educators. He shares his talent, models integrity and generates good will."

Dr. Jody Westbrook
Educational Consultant

To schedule Garre for a keynote address or staff development training

call toll free

1-888-689-3123